THE FAKE NEWS
PHENOMENON

BY DUCHESS HARRIS, JD, PHD

Core Library

An Imprint of Abdo Publishing
abdopublishing.com

Cover image: It's important to view all news reports with a critical eye.

abdopublishing.com

Published by Abdo Publishing, a division of ABDO, PO Box 398166, Minneapolis, Minnesota 55439. Copyright © 2018 by Abdo Consulting Group, Inc. International copyrights reserved in all countries. No part of this book may be reproduced in any form without written permission from the publisher. Core Library™ is a trademark and logo of Abdo Publishing.

Printed in the United States of America, North Mankato, Minnesota
102017
012018

Cover Photo: Shutterstock Images
Interior Photos: Shutterstock Images, 1, 18 (background); Matt McClain/The Washington Post/ Getty Images, 4–5; Sathi Soma/AP Images, 6; Raphael Satter/AP Images, 9; Archiv Gerstenberg/ ullstein bild/Getty Images, 12–13; Niday Picture Library/Alamy, 16–17; iStockphoto, 18 (foreground), 20–21, 36–37, 43; Bettmann/Getty Images, 23; Andrew Harnik/AP Images, 25; A. Araujo/iStockphoto, 28–29; Red Line Editorial, 32; AP Images, 34; M. Spencer Green/ AP Images, 38

Editor: Patrick Donnelly
Imprint Designer: Maggie Villaume
Series Design Direction: Megan Anderson
Contributor: Susan E. Hamen

Publisher's Cataloging-in-Publication Data

Names: Harris, Duchess, author.
Title: The fake news phenomenon / by Duchess Harris.
Description: Minneapolis, Minnesota : Abdo Publishing, 2018. | Series: News literacy | Includes online resources and index.
Identifiers: LCCN 2017947125 | ISBN 9781532113888 (lib.bdg.) | ISBN 9781532152764 (ebook)
Subjects: LCSH: Mass media and public opinion--Juvenile literature. | Journalism--Juvenile literature. | Journalistic ethics--Juvenile literature. | American wit and humor--History and criticism--Juvenile literature.
Classification: DDC 071.309--dc23
LC record available at https://lccn.loc.gov/2017947125

CONTENTS

THE DANGER OF FAKE NEWS

I t was a quiet Sunday afternoon in December 2016 in Washington, DC. At a pizza parlor called Comet Ping Pong, customers enjoyed pizza and played games. Little did they know, their day was about to become very scary.

Shortly before 3:00 p.m., Edgar Maddison Welch entered the restaurant. Welch was 28 years old. He had driven to Washington from Salisbury, North Carolina. As he neared the bar area, Welch raised an assault rifle. He fired a shot toward an employee but missed.

Flowers and signs in support of Comet Ping Pong showed up outside the building in the days following the shooting.

Edgar Maddison Welch surrenders to police after shooting up Comet Ping Pong.

Panic swept through the restaurant. Customers and employees ran for the front door. Welch continued to fire his gun. Bullets ricocheted off walls, a door, and a computer.

Police arrived on the scene. They arrested Welch. The charge was assault with a dangerous weapon.

Nobody was hurt during the incident. But many were very frightened.

What would cause a man to enter a restaurant and open fire? Welch said that he was investigating claims that he'd seen online. He said he had read stories about presidential candidate Hillary Clinton. She was allegedly running a child kidnapping ring out of the restaurant. These stories said children were being sold and abused by adults. None of it was true. Yet the story had been repeated enough that some people believed it. Welch said he visited the restaurant to find out for himself. His investigation quickly turned violent. He surrendered to

PAYING THE PRICE

After the shooting, Welch said he regretted believing the false news stories. Welch was originally charged with assault with a dangerous weapon. He was later charged with more crimes. They included transporting a firearm across state lines. On March 24, 2017, Welch pleaded guilty to two of the charges. He could serve up to seven years in prison.

police when he realized no children were being held captive.

THE RISE OF FAKE NEWS

The false story became known as "Pizzagate." It had circulated for months on social media. It started when e-mails from the Clinton campaign were leaked. Some mentioned Comet Ping Pong's owner, James Alefantis. He supported Clinton in her race against Donald J. Trump. Some people who disliked Clinton created a story. They suggested that the e-mails contained code words for child abuse. These theories were shared on social media. The story grew as it was

Fake news websites that sprung up during the 2016 US presidential race may have influenced some people to not vote for Hillary Clinton.

shared with more people. Some fake news websites picked up the story. That spread the lies even further.

Although the story was completely false, Welch felt he had to investigate. The Pizzagate story shows how fake news can quickly become dangerous. Many people don't know what to believe. All kinds of information can be found on the Internet. Deciding what is true and what isn't can be difficult.

Shortly after Trump's election, a number of fake Twitter accounts were created. These accounts were designed to make the reader think the information being shared was coming from an employee inside the White House. However, most experts believed the accounts were fake.

Social media makes it easier to post and share information. The 2016 presidential election led to a lot of fake news being shared. Supporters of each candidate wanted to influence voters. Spreading unfavorable stories about their opponent was an easy way to do that. But some of those stories were false.

Fake news has become a hot topic in the United States. What news is true? Which news outlets can be trusted? How can media consumers find the answers to these questions? There are ways to tell the difference between real news and fake news. In today's world, it's crucial to know how to spot fake news and stop its spread.

STRAIGHT TO THE
SOURCE

Blogger Alex Jones regularly discussed the kidnapping scam. He apologized after the Comet Ping Pong incident:

In our commentary about what had become known as Pizzagate, I made comments about Mr. Alefantis that in hindsight I regret, and for which I apologize to him. We were participating in a discussion that was being written about by scores of media outlets, in one of the most hotly contested and disputed political environments our country has ever seen. We relied on third-party accounts of alleged activities and conduct at the restaurant. We also relied on accounts of reporters who are no longer with us.

Source: Alex Jones. "A Note to Our Listening, Viewing, and Reading Audiences Concerning Pizzagate Coverage." *InfoWars*. InfoWars, 2017. Web. Accessed April 14, 2017.

Point of View

Jones said he regrets promoting the Pizzagate story. What reasons does he provide for discussing the story? Do you believe they are legitimate? Make sure you explain your opinion. Include facts and details that support your reasons.

CHAPTER TWO

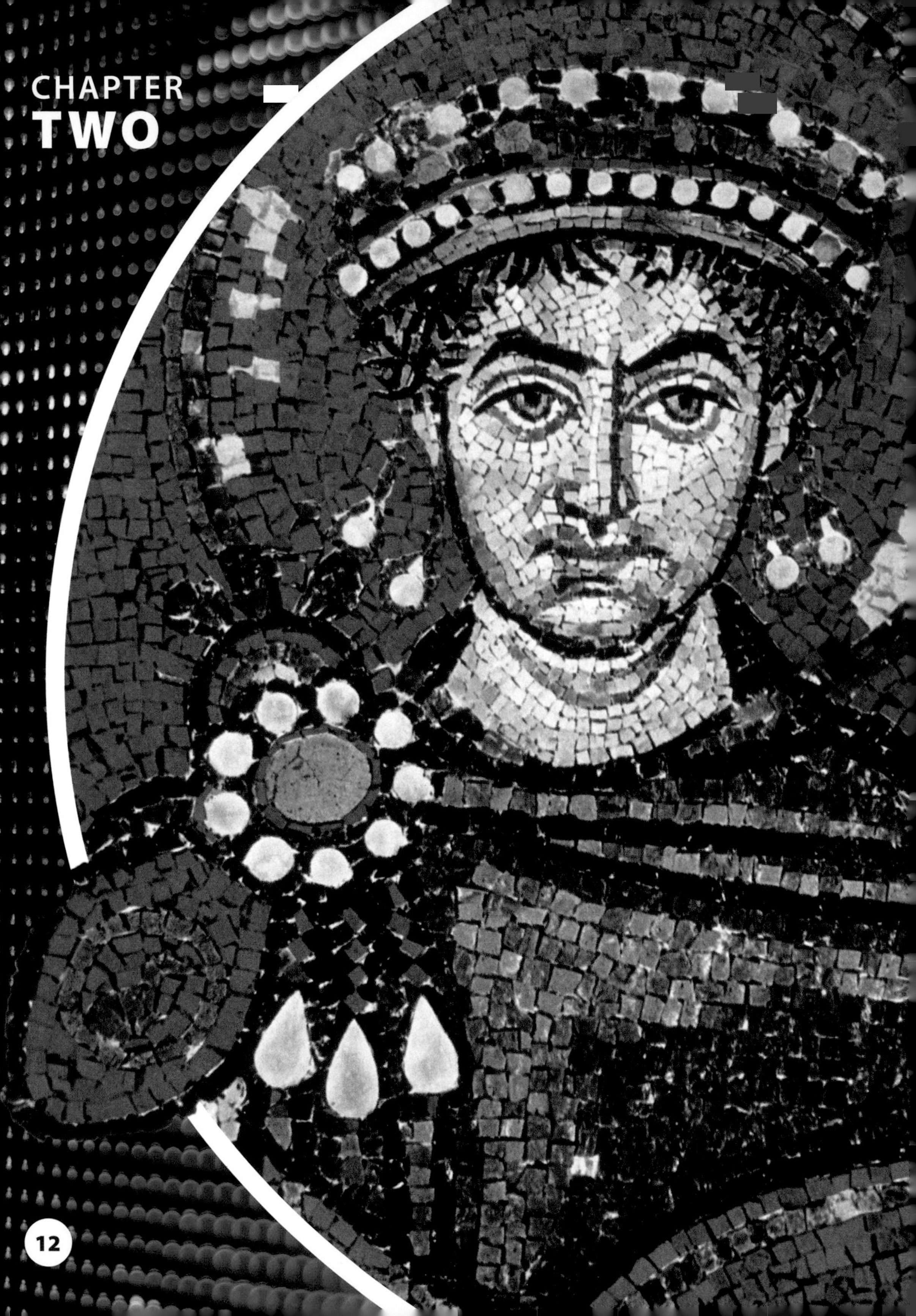

HISTORY OF FAKE NEWS

Fake news is any false story that looks like news. It is designed to convince readers that it's true. Some fake news is created and spread intentionally. A poorly researched story that contains errors might also be considered fake news. Fake news has boomed in recent years. But it is not a new concept. In fact, it has been around for more than 1,500 years.

LIES AGAINST LEADERS

Procopius was a historian of the 500s CE. He lived in what is now Israel. He is considered responsible for some of the earliest fake news.

Emperor Justinian was one of the early rulers who benefited from Procopius's reporting.

Procopius served as a military adviser before returning to the region's capital, Constantinople. He recorded details about wars and building projects. He also wrote glorified stories about Emperor Justinian and other important politicians. But after Procopius died, more of his writings were found. These hidden articles, known as *Anecdota*, told a much different story about political leaders. They were damaging to Emperor Justinian's reputation. It's impossible to know which of the stories were true and which were exaggerated or false.

PASQUINADES

In 1522 Italian author Pietro Aretino tried to influence the election of the next Pope. He wrote scandalous poems about all the candidates except his favorite. He pasted them on a statue local residents had named "Pasquino." It was located in a town square in Rome. All who passed by could read the false claims about the candidates. His poems became known as "pasquinades."

The 1600s saw a spike in fake news. In this era, the invention of the printing press made mass printing possible. Papers with outlandish fake news stories were printed and sold on the streets of Paris, France. They were known as "canards." During the French Revolution (1789–1799), political canards were sold throughout Paris. They helped fuel dislike toward the queen, Marie Antoinette. The

The French people revolted against the monarchy, fueled in part by fake news "canards" spread throughout Paris.

public's hatred grew. Eventually, she was imprisoned and executed.

GOSSIP GOES TO PRINT

The trend carried over to London as well. By 1788 London was home to nearly 30 newspapers. The stories

in many of these papers consisted of gossip overheard by writers. Newspaper publishers did not care if the stories were true. The public loved to read gossip. Rival newspapers tried to outdo each other. They printed even more scandalous stories.

INFORMATION
OVERLOAD

A flood of information is exchanged on social media every day. Nobody knows how much of it is fake, but it's clear that users click on, forward, repost, and tweet fake news millions of times a day. Many have good intentions. They simply don't realize the news they're sharing isn't truthful. What does that tell you about how fake news has spread since social media became prevalent?

FACEBOOK
4.75 billion pieces of information shared daily

YOUTUBE
432,000 hours of video uploaded every day

TWITTER
500 million tweets sent per day

As the United States grew, so did its exposure to fake news. In the late 1800s, competing New York City newspapers tried to outsell each other. Reporters began embellishing stories to draw attention and sell papers. These tactics became known as "yellow journalism." One example came in 1898. Cuba was in revolt against Spain. The USS *Maine* was sent to Cuba to protect American interests there. It sank near Havana. Some newspaper publishers saw this as an opportunity for attention. They rushed to blame Spain. They spun exaggerated or false stories that fed on the public's fear and outrage. Soon many Americans were demanding revenge. Within months, the United States was at war with Spain.

FAKE NEWS IN THE MODERN WORLD

Unfortunately, fake news is not something of the past. Many people today struggle to sort fact from fiction. According to one report, nearly two-thirds of American adults believe that fake news causes confusion about current events and issues.

WHY LIE?

Social media isn't the only source of fake news. Personal blogs often spread misinformation. Tabloid magazines spread rumors to sell copies to curious fans of celebrities. Some television and talk radio programs take sides. They may ignore news they are biased against. Even some newspapers report news that is later proved untrue.

News articles aren't the only items the public should question. Photos can be just as suspect on the Internet. For many, seeing is believing. But photo editing software allows users to make fake images.

With so many options to pick from, it can be difficult to know which media sources to trust.

PUSHING AN AGENDA

Fake news often is created to support one side of an argument. The Pizzagate story is a good example. It was created to make the Clinton campaign look bad. Fake news became a widespread talking point during and after the 2016 presidential election. The Internet was abuzz with fake news stories. Some were spread by the candidates' supporters. Others were created to make money through web advertising.

Propaganda is another form of fake news. It is created by governments to mislead or misinform citizens. Propaganda has been an effective tool. During World War II (1939–1945), the Nazi Party used it. They wanted to influence German citizens' opinions and attitudes about Jews. The Nazis used scare tactics that warned about false dangers the Jews presented. That propaganda helped turn ordinary citizens against their fellow Germans.

Propaganda was part of the Nazi plan to turn public sentiment against Jewish people in Germany.

Juden in BERLIN

NO PAY TO PLAY

One widely shared story claimed that Clinton paid entertainers Beyoncé and Jay Z $62 million to perform at a rally. The article claimed that Clinton was desperate to get more African-American votes. It said she paid the celebrities to endorse her. The story was proven false. But the lie had already affected the way some people thought of Clinton. One tweet suggested that the fake news worked. The user wrote, "Hillary Clinton paid $62 million to Jay Z and Beyonce . . . while our Vets go hungry and homeless."

Because they believed the propaganda, German citizens looked the other way as Jews were forced out of their homes and taken to concentration camps. An estimated 6 million Jews were murdered in what came to be known as the Holocaust.

SHOCK VALUE

We live in the information age. News is always

Beyoncé and Jay Z did campaign for Hillary Clinton in 2016, but not because she paid them $62 million as alleged by one fake news story.

quickly available. But people are drawn to shocking stories. Many headlines are written as teases to entice people to click on them. When people follow this "clickbait," they may be taken to advertisements rather than actual news articles.

Some online writers are not paid per article or per word. Instead, they are paid based on how many pageviews their articles get. The more times people click on the links to their articles, the more money the writer makes. Therefore, they want their headlines to be as tempting as possible. They exaggerate, embellish, or lie to get clicks.

STRAIGHT TO THE
SOURCE

Writer Farhad Manjoo argues that technological advancements have made it harder to tell fact from fiction.

> *More than a decade ago . . . [t]he internet was filled with 9/11 truthers, and partisans who believed against all evidence that George W. Bush stole the 2004 election from John Kerry, or that Barack Obama was a foreign-born Muslim. . . . Of course, America has long been entranced by conspiracy theories. But the online hoaxes and fringe theories appeared more virulent than their offline predecessors. They were also more numerous and more persistent. During Mr. Obama's 2008 presidential campaign, every attempt to debunk the birther rumor seemed to raise its prevalence online.*

> Source: Farhad Manjoo. "How the Internet Is Loosening Our Grip on the Truth." *New York Times*. New York Times, November 2, 2016. Web. Accessed July 12, 2017.

What's the Big Idea?

Take a close look at this passage. What is the main connection being made between technology and the spread of fake news? What does the writer say about our willingness to embrace conspiracies and other fake news? Do you agree with him? Why or why not?

CHAPTER
FOUR

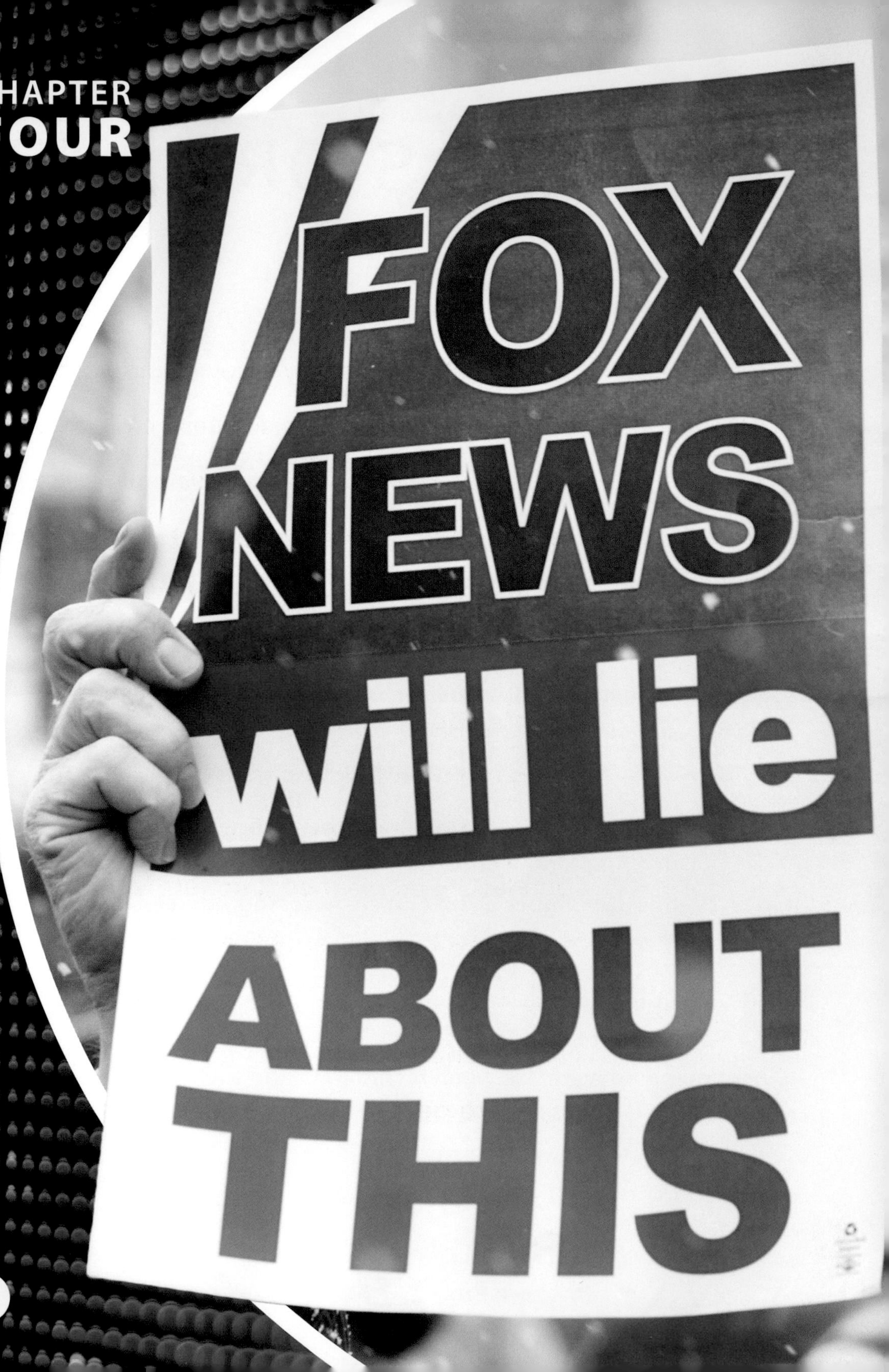

BIAS OR LIES?

Some television channels present news 24 hours a day. They include cable news networks such as Fox News, CNN, and MSNBC. These news outlets are dedicated to broadcasting news. But that does not mean they are necessarily trustworthy.

Some news outlets report in a way that is more appealing to their audience. Some stations have a liberal slant. Others are more conservative. Fox News, for example, was founded by media mogul Rupert Murdoch. He hired a former Republican Party media consultant to run the channel. As a result, Fox News stories tend to favor conservatives. They appeal to people who support Republican

A protester in Wisconsin makes his feelings known about Fox News.

ideas and political candidates. Meanwhile, many Democrats prefer MSNBC's reporting. It carries more of a liberal bias.

Most news sources want to provide information. Some also want to persuade their audience. It is possible to do both. For example, newspapers tend to report straight news. They want to inform rather than persuade. But most newspapers also include opinion and editorial pieces. These articles are written by writers, readers, and editors. They offer an opinion on the topics of the day. Television and radio news stations employ anchors and hosts who present the news. But some also offer their opinions.

SKEWING THE FACTS

When news sources skew their reporting, the result is bias. Bias is unfair favoritism toward one side of an issue. When different news stations report the same news story, the facts may be presented differently. Fox News might present a story on President Trump with a positive spin. Meanwhile, MSNBC might report the same story but portray Trump negatively. Why would news outlets skew the facts? It is often done to satisfy their audiences.

Sometimes news sources will report the facts accurately but will then draw political conclusions. The line between information and opinion becomes blurry. Viewers and listeners are being told what to think. This is not truly fake news.

ADDRESSING THE DANGERS OF FAKE NEWS

After the events of the Pizzagate shooting, Clinton spoke out about the dangers of fake news. "This is not about politics or partisanship. Lives are at risk, lives of ordinary people just trying to go about their days to do their jobs, contribute to their communities," Clinton said. "It is a danger that must be addressed and addressed quickly."

But if people only hear one side of an issue, they are more likely to believe false reports about the other side. Their views become skewed because of what they

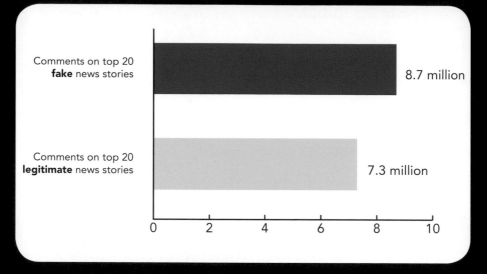

FAKE NEWS GETS VIEWS

Comments on top 20 **fake** news stories — 8.7 million

Comments on top 20 **legitimate** news stories — 7.3 million

0 2 4 6 8 10

In the final three months of the 2016 presidential election, the top 20 fake news stories on Facebook drew more comments than the top 20 stories pulled from 19 mainstream news sites. Why do you think that happened? What does that say about the power of fake news? Do you think it had an impact on the election?

have heard. It then becomes easier to believe fake news stories.

Just before the 2016 election, a story emerged about teenagers in Macedonia. They were making money by creating fake news articles about US politics. One report found more than 100 pro-Trump fake news websites being operated out of one city. The teens said they made the most money from Trump supporters clicking on anti-Clinton fake news articles. The articles may have damaged some people's opinion of Clinton.

WHAT ABOUT ALTERNATIVE FACTS?

In January 2017, White House press secretary Sean Spicer said the crowd at President Trump's inauguration was the largest

ever. This was proved to be false. When asked why Spicer lied, Trump's senior adviser Kellyanne Conway

> **Donald J. Trump** ✔
> @realDonaldTrump
>
> `Following`
>
> It is the same Fake News Media that said there is "no path to victory for Trump" that is now pushing the phony Russia story. A total scam!
>
> RETWEETS LIKES
> 22,581   87,127
>
> 6:02 AM - 1 Apr 2017

Donald Trump used social media to accuse the mainstream media of promoting fake news.

explained, "You're saying it's a falsehood. And [he] . . . gave alternative facts."

Conway's answer sparked new debate regarding fake news. What are alternative facts? Are facts up for debate? Are alternative facts simply lies? Chuck Todd of NBC News thought so. He responded to Conway, saying, "Alternative facts aren't facts, they are falsehoods."

WHAT FAKE NEWS IS NOT

The term *fake news* refers to fictional stories. However, some have attempted to give it a new definition. During

Trump's first 100 days as president, he accused some news outlets of reporting fake news about him. These articles reported unfavorable news.

But that didn't mean the articles were not true. Just because a politician or celebrity is unhappy about a story does not mean it is fake news. With the term *fake news* being used more and more, it can be difficult to know what to believe. Fortunately, with a little work, it is possible to find the truth.

FURTHER EVIDENCE

Chapter Four covers information about fake news in reporting. What was one of the main points of this chapter? What evidence supports this point? Read the article at the website below. Does the information on the website support the main point of the chapter? Does it present new evidence?

READING, WRITING, AND FIGHTING FAKE NEWS
abdocorelibrary.com/fake-news

CHAPTER FIVE

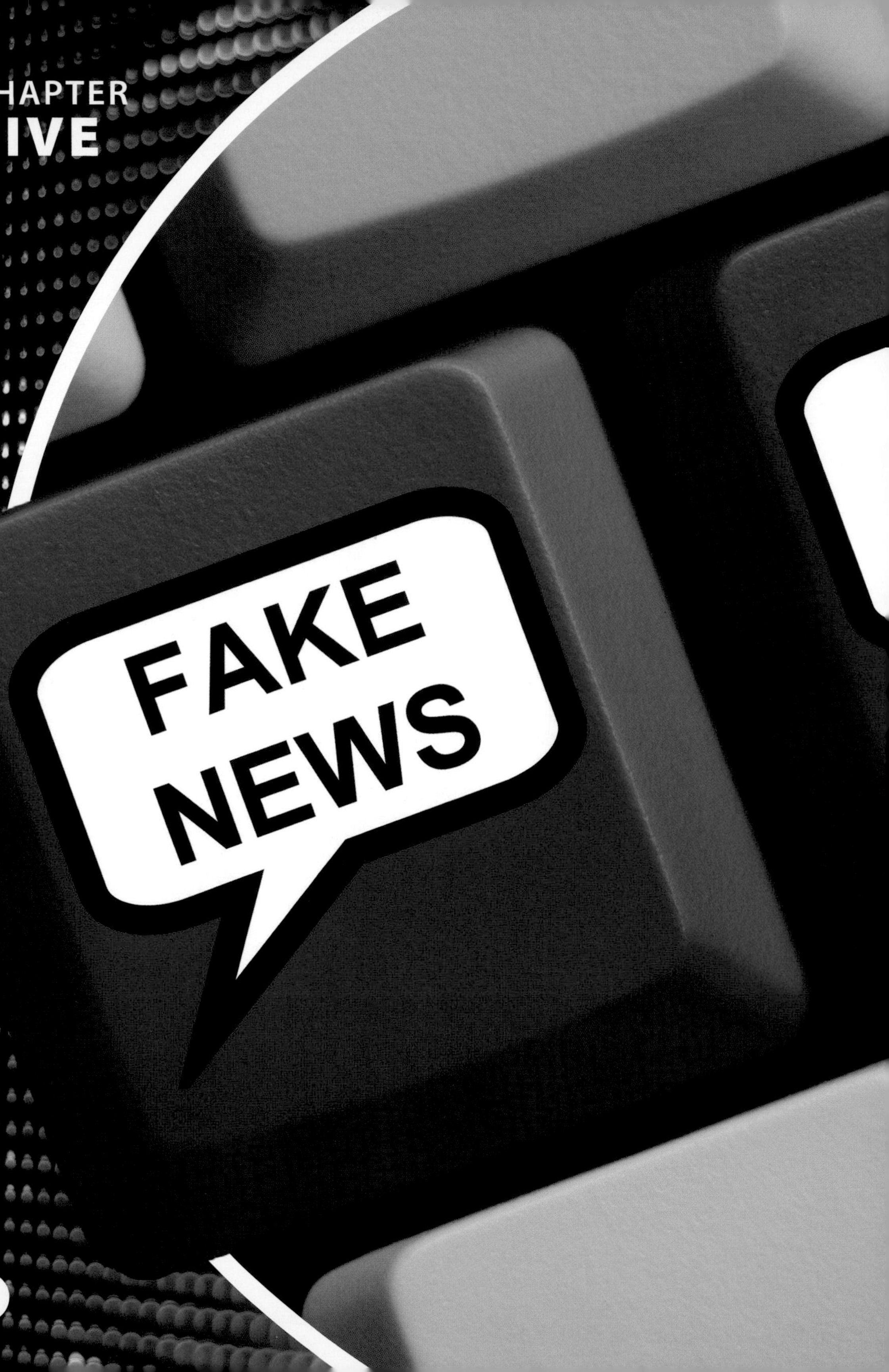

SPOTTING FAKE NEWS

Fake news is nearly impossible to avoid. So how can people decide whether to trust a news source? Schools have begun teaching students about news literacy. News literacy involves using critical thinking to examine the news you read and hear. It's everyone's job to dig deeper and do research to determine a news report's credibility.

TIPS FOR IDENTIFYING FAKE NEWS

A lot of fake news appears online. Inspecting the website where a story is posted can reveal

If only it were as simple as tapping a few keys to distinguish real news from fake. However, there are some steps you can take to get better results.

A woman shares a copy of the *Chicago Defender* with police officers the morning after Barack Obama won the 2008 presidential election. Many minority communities have their own newspapers that cover issues of importance to them.

clues about whether the source is trustworthy. Some popular websites are known to be biased. Fact-checking sites list known fake news sites.

Look to see if the author provides his or her credentials. Perform a Web search to see if the author has written other articles. If you're unable to find information about the author, be cautious.

Trustworthy news articles will provide sources for facts and figures. Be skeptical of articles that offer data without backing it up with a legitimate source. Check the domain of the website hosting the article. Website URLs that end with *.edu* are connected to a school or university. Those that end with *.gov* are used for government websites. These tend to be more trustworthy. The *.com* and *.net* web addresses can be created by anyone. They should be carefully investigated for accuracy.

Another big fake news tip-off is poor writing. Real news websites use professional writers and editors.

NEWS SOURCE OPTIONS

Mainstream media sources aren't the only places people get their news. Some communities rely on different outlets to stay informed. Many minority communities even have their own press. The *Chicago Defender*, for example, is Chicago's oldest African-American newspaper. The *Defender* is a weekly newspaper and online news source that was founded in 1905.

Their articles are less likely to contain bad grammar and typos. If you have found an article that is poorly written, chances are it wasn't written by a professional.

Websites such as FactCheck.org and Politifact investigate stories for inaccuracy. Check to see if the story you're reading or hearing appears on one of these websites.

STOPPING THE SPREAD

Facebook has taken a stand against the spread of fake news. It has partnered with fact-checking organizations to flag disputed articles. The warning advises readers that a reliable source has noted the article is fake. This allows the reader to proceed with caution. They can check the facts before accepting the article as true and sharing it with others.

Stopping the spread of fake news is just as important as learning to spot it. Before sharing, investigate a news story using other sources. Do some basic detective work to help decide if the story is true, partially true, or completely fake. Don't be part of the problem by blindly sharing everything you read on social media.

EXPLORE ONLINE

Chapter Five offers ways to spot fake news. The article at the website below goes into more depth on this topic. What new information does the website present?

THE CLASSROOM WHERE FAKE NEWS FAILS
abdocorelibrary.com/fake-news

FAST FACTS

- Fake news has been around for at least 1,500 years.

- So-called "yellow journalism" was blamed for inciting the Spanish-American War in 1898.

- Social media makes it easier to share all types of information, including fake news.

- The 2016 presidential election led to a dramatic increase in fake news.

- Teenagers in Macedonia made money by creating hundreds of fake news websites during the 2016 presidential campaign. The most lucrative were anti–Hillary Clinton sites.

- In December 2016 a man shot up a pizza parlor because he believed a fake news story that said it was the headquarters of a child kidnapping ring. He was sentenced to seven years in prison.

- Fact-checking sites can help readers determine which news outlets are legitimate and which are fake.

- Nearly two-thirds of American adults believe that fake news causes confusion about current events and issues.

STOP AND
THINK

Tell the Tale

Chapter One discusses the story of a man who stormed a restaurant with a gun because he'd been fooled by a fake news story. How do you think you might feel if you suddenly realized a news story was fake? Write 200 words about your experience. How might it affect your future willingness to believe news stories?

Surprise Me

Chapter Two discusses the history of fake news. After reading this book, what two or three facts about fake news did you find most surprising? Write a few sentences about each fact. Why did you find each fact surprising?

Dig Deeper

After reading this book, what questions do you still have about fake news? With an adult's help, find a few reliable sources that can help you answer your questions. Write a paragraph about what you learned.

GLOSSARY

agenda
the plan or motives of a group or person

bias
favoring one side over another

candidate
a person who is competing for a job or position

clickbait
an exaggerated or false headline meant to entice people to read a story

conservative
supportive of traditional ways of doing things

credibility
believability

fact-check
investigate in an attempt to verify details of a news story

liberal
open to new ways of doing things

partisan
a supporter of a group or cause

propaganda
information that is misleading and is used to change the public's point of view about something

skew
to distort something

ONLINE
RESOURCES

To learn more about fake news, visit our free resource websites below.

Visit **abdocorelibrary.com** for free Common Core resources for teachers and students, including vetted activities, multimedia, and booklinks, for deeper subject comprehension.

Visit **abdobooklinks.com** for free additional online weblinks for further learning. These links are routinely monitored and updated to provide the most current information available.

LEARN
MORE

Hand, Carol. *How the Internet Changed History*. Minneapolis, MN: Abdo Publishing, 2015.

Hurt, Avery Elizabeth, ed. *Trial By Internet*. New York: Greenhaven Publishing, 2017.

ABOUT THE
AUTHOR

Duchess Harris, JD, PhD
Professor Harris is the chair of the American Studies Department at Macalester College. The author and coauthor of four books (*Hidden Human Computers: The Black Women of NASA* and *Black Lives Matter* with Sue Bradford Edwards, *Racially Writing the Republic: Racists, Race Rebels, and Transformations of American Identity* with Bruce Baum, and *Black Feminist Politics from Kennedy to Clinton/Obama*), she has been an associate editor for *Litigation News*, the American Bar Association Section's quarterly flagship publication, and was the first editor-in-chief of *Law Raza Journal*, an interactive online race and the law journal for William Mitchell College of Law.

She has earned a PhD in American Studies from the University of Minnesota and a Juris Doctorate from William Mitchell College of Law.

INDEX